JONATHAN HARVEY

Song Offerings

for soprano and 8 instrumentalists

(1985)

Text from *Gitanjali* by Rabindranath Tagore
translated by himself

Faber Music Limited
London

© 1988 by Faber Music Ltd
First published in 1988 by Faber Music Ltd
3 Queen Square London WC1N 3AU
Music drawn by Paul Broom
Cover design by M & S Tucker
Printed in England by Loader Jackson Printers Ltd

Cover illustration: Illustration to 'Gita Govinda',
Kangra School, late eighteenth century.
(Prince of Wales Museum, Bombay)

Words from *Gitanjali* by Rabindranath Tagore (47, 57, 56, 91)
translated by himself
Text © 1967 Trustees of the Rabindranath Tagore Estate
and Macmillan Publishers

Song Offerings was commissioned by Spectrum
with funds provided by the Arts Council of Great Britain,
and first performed by Spectrum with Rosemary Hardy, soprano,
conducted by Guy Protheroe, at the Queen Elizabeth Hall,
London, on 22 March 1985

Duration: c. 17 minutes

INSTRUMENTATION

Flute/Alto flute
Clarinet in B♭
2 Violins
Viola
Cello
Doublebass (doubling Crotale)
Piano

The crotale must be pitched

The Doublebass must have a low C extension

NOTATION

✝ = 1/4 tone sharp
♯♯ = 3/4 tone sharp
ⓓ = 1/4 tone flat
ⓓ♭ = 3/4 tone flat
↓ = very slightly flat
+ = l. h. pizzicato
▲ = highest possible note

For Ann and Guy

SONG OFFERINGS

for soprano and eight instrumentalists

JONATHAN HARVEY

I

open to him — forbid him not.   If the sound of his steps does not wake me, do not try to rouse me, I pray.   I wish not to be

called by the clamorous choir of birds,   by the ri-ot of   wind at the festival of morning light.   Let

first of all lights and all forms. _____ The first thrill of joy — to my awakened soul

let it come__ from his glance. _____ And let my re - turn to my -

attacca!

* Strings: accelerate tremolandi al fine

II

8

movendo

a tempo, ma vivo

14

16

and it scatters gems— in — pro - fu - sion.

III

21

† Fl. fingering
bar 6 :

22

24

25

26

30

32

IV

* Strings: ⌇⌇⌇ = vibrato pulse - an accentuation made solely by faster, wider vibrato

38

*Three of the four with whistled notes should be chosen by the conductor

have ever flowed towards thee in depth of secrecy.

(spoken freely)

One final glance from thine eyes and my life will be ever thine own.

42

44